The Editors

Minnu Ann Stanly

Mitreyi Venugopal

Anoshka Maria Heri

I've been frequently asked this question. Why do you write? I've never had a particular reply to this; each time I described a poem; I would choose the context nearest to it. This seemed like the best possible way of handling this question. But I wouldn't be happy with what I've said; it made me sad and rather worthless because I couldn't figure out the very thing that I regretted the most.

I gradually realized that I was destined to write. It wasn't something that surfaced overnight; it happened over the years of muffled thoughts that amalgamated inside me. But then I also feel like I write for a greater purpose, something that I do not understand. I write for all the people who do not enjoy the act of writing something down because life has consumed them a lot, or maybe they just don't understand the concept of documenting torment. Yet, I believe there's no way I could represent such a huge crowd. I'd rather write for something more abstract than humans; I write for torment.

I can never agree with myself about certain things; I can never reach a conclusion; maybe I just don't want to, and therefore, I'll never really know why I write.

Umber Oblivion

OrangeBooks Publication

1st Floor, Rajhans Arcade, Mall Road, Kohka, Bhilai, Chhattisgarh 490020
Website: **www.orangebooks.in**

© **Copyright, 2025, Author**

All rights reserved. No part of this book may be reproduced, stored in a retrieval system, or transmitted in any form by any means, electronic, mechanical, magnetic, optical, chemical, manual, photocopying, recording or otherwise, without the prior written consent of its writer.

First Edition, 2025

ISBN: 978-93-6554-942-3

UMBER OBLIVION

ROMIL UDAYAKUMAR TNV

OrangeBooks Publication
www.orangebooks.in

स्वागत

Swaagat

I've written this for over four years. To me, it wasn't even a book when I started writing it; it was just a seventeen-year-old boy learning words that would later rearrange themselves into his reflection. Now that I've completed it, it just doesn't become a book; it is a manifestation, nothing magical; it is memories blended around in an umber boy's reality. An oblivion was later created around it when I tried to jot it down.

Umber Oblivion is not just a book; it is everybody who contributed to its being: everybody who dragged me, everybody who lifted me, everybody who taught me how to love. Now that I try to etch this oblivion's being in time, I forewarn you that as you walk along this road of mine, you won't find what you hope for, but you will find a chaotic solitude amongst these memories of mine. It may be redundant; it may be too dark at times or too corny, but it is the nearest witness to an unworthy life, unworthy of knowing.

Yet what troubles me the most is the absence of these words in my nightmares, which sometimes come over, piercing the sheath of reality I've created, and so I battle the very creatures I've created. I present to you the "UMBER OBLIVION."

Contents

Chapter - 1
 The Pencil Car 1

Chapter - 2
 Almost Not A Toddler 10

Chapter - 3
 IV-G..15

Chapter - 4
 Hunting Escapism 19

Chapter - 5
 Nalla Kutty 26

Chapter - 6
 Old Friend 28

Chapter - 7
 Mirage...31

Chapter - 8
 Dopamine...37

Chapter - 9
 Papa...41

Chapter - 10
 The Man In The Sky 45

Chapter - 11
  Adrenaline Hunger 54

Chapter - 12
  Walk Way 62

Chapter - 13
  Ocean Eyes 68

Chapter - 14
  Merry Christmas 81

Chapter - 15
  Gaia 85

Chapter - 16
  Snap Back To Reality 90

Chapter - 17
  Even Tide 98

Chapter - 18
  Homeless 101

Chapter - 19
  Strange But Home 103

Chapter - 20
  Homeland 107

Chapter - 21
  Tears In Heaven 110

Chapter - 22
  Lucy 116

Chapter - 23
　　Internet Heroes 122

Chapter - 24
　　What Is God? 126

Chapter - 25
　　Death? 133

Chapter - 26
　　I Haven't Lived 139

Chapter - 1
The Pencil Car

Heartbreaks have followed me throughout my life; they've been redundant and clingy, and maybe that is why I remember each of those moments vibrantly like it all happened yesterday. I went shopping with Mummy at Dhiraj Sons. Mummy never really got me toys; she had other bills to pay, so I scoured around to look for toys I'd get for free. There was a bottle of Horlicks that gave away this blue pencil box car that I had absolutely loved. I took it home, looked at it, and admired it, and that's all I could think about for a while. I woke up early the next day, sharpened all the pencils that I had, and gently placed them in my precious race car pencil box.

I had to attend the coaching classes right before I went to school since Mummy was a teacher, and she had to be there early. I was excited, happy, and maybe even proud that I had that pencil box with me. I walked into the coaching class, sat down with a smile, and took my race car out with lots of pride. I smirked at my friends sitting around me. All of a sudden, I felt this warmth around my face, which kind of shot up and startled me. I looked at what did that, and before I could turn around, I got a second slap right across my face.

I couldn't really figure out what I did because I was always told to take a beating, and I kept telling myself I might have done something wrong. Just as I was figuring things out, I heard a bang. The woman banged my favorite race car pencil box on the table, and all the things that I had gently placed in it flew out. I immediately crouched to duck the slaps coming my way and to save those pencils that I had spent a lot of time on. As I knelt down to pick up the pencil from under the table, I stretched my neck and hand simultaneously as I left a trail of tears that I tried to hide, but my body wouldn't cooperate and kept hyperventilating. I grieved even looking at the dented axle of my broken race car. That very moment is the first memory of a heartbreak I couldn't get over for months, and yet I couldn't really talk about it.

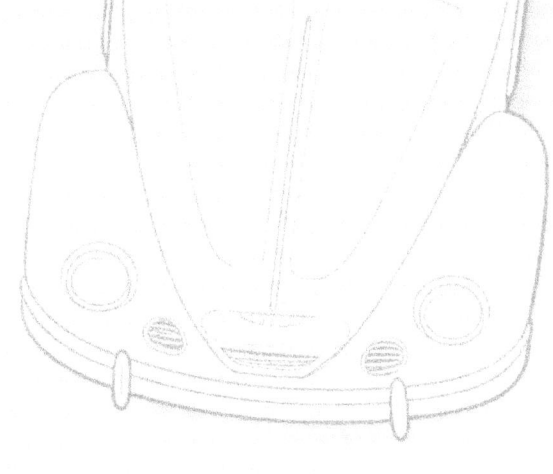

TWAS ONCE A CHILD

I see a distressed man mumbling in the shadows.

He was chained and shackled to the gallows.
Then, my eyes conjured a child

A child running through a meadow,
A meadow so fine and green feels as though
Somewhere, some place I have been,
He looks at me and darts into a valley.
A valley so deep, so serene.

There flows a stream oh so bright,
It looked like a spit of sunlight.
The valley turned direfully grim.

The sky turned red; it sang an obsequious hymn.

The child gazed into my eyes as the man slit his throat.
His chains were wet with gore.
His spirit grew frail and sore.
But when I gazed into his eyes,
I felt as though it was my reflection that he bore.

Claws And Petrichor

For when I go grey and forget what life was.

*Would I still be in pain, hoping and waiting for
these covert memories?
Dreaming of a child in love being raised
Reminiscing my youth, the sunsets I've chased
That would be an oblivion of complete turmoil.*

*My mind reminds me of the soil.
I lie down and lose myself in this reverie.
My eyes lead me to pain.
But my heart dreams of petrichor and rain.*

Who would I be?

*The world would remain the same.
But what would I see?
Would I be someone else?
Or would I still be me?*

I fear that I might exist differently.
I was forged with flaws.
I'd have the same mortal soul
yet birthing immortal foes.

I toiled over, detested manly laws.
But now that I create a new being,

I still feel the claws.

Under His Wing

We are all jailed in this labyrinthine.

*For I was introduced to a god that could
turn water into wine.*
*We all gathered and hoped to perish then
transcend into a place so divine.*
*Salvation Salvation, they exclaimed,
"He will come the second time."*

I'm just as human as he is.

But the almighty deemed differently, it seemed.
Sedated into a fancied cosmic trance.
*Thou shalt praise the redeemer,
and thou shalt be redeemed.*

I will look into your disillusioned eyes.

When you realize man made God and his beautiful lies
All for the government and its ties
For nobody listens to us, our grief or blaring cries.

Will you live one day?

Or will you watch your life inch off of your grip and slip away?
For the Saviour, don't love you no more.
But under his wings, he wants you to stay.

Umber Oblivion

Chapter – 2
Almost Not A Toddler

I have ample memories of loneliness and agony. These are feeble nuances, yet they linger around like that scar you get on your brow; they stay till you croak.

Well, nobody accompanied me to the park. I ran down the street and waited till an autorickshaw filled with passengers arrived. They cost less, and I was pocket-sized; I'd fit right about anywhere. I loved sitting beside the driver; it made me feel like a big boy, and the polluted breeze that blew over my face was comforting. As soon as we reach, I'll jump down and hand the driver a five rupee note. I'd run to the school gate, wave at the watchman and walk in, in anticipation.

I stroll around the school campus, wandering along the ground, hoping I'd find somebody to play with. Even though I couldn't hear what those parents whispered inside their kids' ears, by the looks they gave me, I did understand that they wouldn't like their kids to be with the likes of me. Well, who would want their kids to play with a child from a broken home? I'd walk around the place with a toddler's head filled with misery; I believe those were my first experiences of desolation.

I stuck around after church to hang out with my friends. I was a good Christian boy. I took part in the choir and arranged the dais, and then when all the decals left, I and my friends ran around the benches chasing each other. We quarreled, we fought, and we did everything we could to incite chaos. I was ten at the time, and silence was rather uncomfortable unless people were chasing me or me chasing them around. I was only really doing what my high-energy kid cognition was telling me. I did have a good time, yet shadowing all of it was a memory of a friend. I was running around him, and we were pretending to be wrestlers. I got him in a headlock, and that's when he looked me dead in the eye and asked me where my father was and why he was away. Adolescent me understands that he did not say that to dent my feelings; it was like a low blow. I must say he did succeed. Shadowing all these memories of chaos are those two questions where and why.

Juvenile Messiah

I looked at the sun and wondered

What if I was God for one day,
Everything would work my way,
In sweet paradise would I stay,
On these empty promises called clouds, I lay.
Nobody would go home hungry
No promises would be broken,
No lives would be taken,
The sick will be cured and the crippled will be risen,
The blind will see, and the deaf will listen,
Nobody a beggar
Nobody a lord,
No war, no cries
No cries, no sword
No exploitation, no scam, no fraud,

Wouldn't all this be a hoax,
A stupid teenage paradox.
All this is just a dream,
Completely hopeless and fictional, as it seems.
As into the harsh reality I lean,

Well, nobody could be a God,
No miracles done,
No events foreseen,
I'd a good man Ma taught me to be,
Till I cease to breathe and tenderly slumber in the green.

Chapter - 3

IV-G

Even though I despise my life a lot, I sometimes want to live it once again or just want to watch myself live from a distance so that I can see the joy on my face and on the faces of the people I love. I would love my life so much that if I could, I'd deny slumber and choose joy over it. Those moments of bliss are really rare in my life, perhaps because I can't recall them as vividly as I recall trauma.

It was the annual sports meet. I was in 4th grade, and I was quite an athletic kid. I won around 5 medals. I couldn't be happier, I guess. That moment when every classmate of mine looked at me as though I had superpowers. We all sat down in the classroom after the sports meet, and we were all ready to get the medals. I looked right at the medals, and as time passed, I kept getting agitated about receiving what I had rightfully earned.

Ambily ma'am took her sweet time to appreciate each of the students that won that day, and at last, she kept stalling; she wouldn't call my name, and everyone looked at me in anticipation. I kept looking at Ambily Ma'am, waiting for her to call my name, and she kept looking around; she kept teasing me, and my anticipation turned into weariness. Then she looked at everyone, with a wide smile on her face, and said, I smell something burning. Everyone looked at me and laughed, and I did too. She knew I was weary, but it was just too darn funny. Later, she called me in front and placed a bunch of those medals on my neck. At that moment, everything else sank under the sound of applause, and that moment was bliss.

I Live In Malice

I wish my eyes never grew in life.
I wish I could still feel magic.
I wish I could awe at the clouds.

I wish this torment were impaled, for
I long for a seraphic knife.

I've seen time wear down promises.
Promises that eventually die
I've seen death and sorrow, love and lies,
torture and tribulation.

I wish I could borrow your grief,
but all I could do was exult that quietus sigh.
My eyes still wake up to your muffled cries.

But the murky night conceals it with lies.

My heart that still thuds buried under malice
Craves for life, yet I gently grin as it sedately dies.

I'd still smother a dream if I live.
I'd still rejoice at gore.
I'd still unlearn to forgive.

For when I die, my heart still thuds, my soul grieves.
The flesh amends, yet the malice lives.

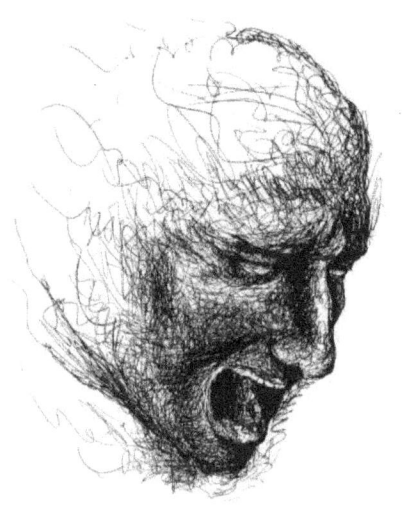

Chapter - 4
Hunting Escapism

Noel and I searched for every coin we could collect to sneak out to the gaming center, 'Om's Game World'. We had the time of our lives. It was this place in a basement right behind a tea stall, and next to it was a toner cartridge shop, so each time I hopped down those stairs excited to play, I could smell fresh ink and tobacco. I pushed the door open to find paradise, and the best part of it was that it never changed places; I just needed enough money. The PlayStation 2 costs 30 rupees for an hour. We sat there for the first 15 minutes, killing time, listening to the kids ramble cuss words at the screen. It was fun.

This was the place where all kinds of kids could come in, and we did not know there was a line before, but it's been displayed that there is, in fact, one. The impoverished kids would walk in; they had shabby clothes, murky golden-colored hair, and dirty teeth. They came in, handed over the money, and sat where they felt like sitting. I really admired how they behaved, as though nothing around them could cause consequences they could not handle; it was rather too rogue for 12-year-old me. I'd sometimes sit next to them, curious about how they behaved. I sat there, learning how they react to and talk about things. Each time they walked in, they had to discuss how they'd eat if they played for an hour. It was not a conversation I had with my brother; there was always food when we went back home, so pretty much everything that they did intrigued me.

I walked into the shop alone for a project I had to do. I paid for the computer, and right next to me was a child as old as me but smaller, shabbier, and thinner. He had these huge headphones over his head and was listening to music as he played Grand Theft Auto. He then gently took out a piece of rag from his pocket. It crumbled and looked as if it hadn't been washed for years. He then proceeded to take out a tube of superglue. He rubbed it on the rag and sniffed it for a couple of seconds. I did not understand what he was doing, but I knew it wasn't good. I could see that boy fall into a trance, and I could feel him get dizzy. That's when I flinched, and the owner slapped the kid right on the back of his head. He fell onto the keyboard and was then thrown out of the shop, yet he had that grin, the grin you have when you're told not to do something but you still do it, and then it brings you this weird kind of happiness. I've thought about that very scenario multiple times. I was now aware that there existed a line that differentiated humans from poor humans; they did not even try to hide it; it was right in front of us, evident to all that lives on this planet. I did understand that one could behave differently towards different human beings. I wasn't exactly desolate right when this happened, but I am, at times, thinking of life on stale bread and super glue. I've realized how minuscule my effects on this detrimental world are.

Umber Oblivion

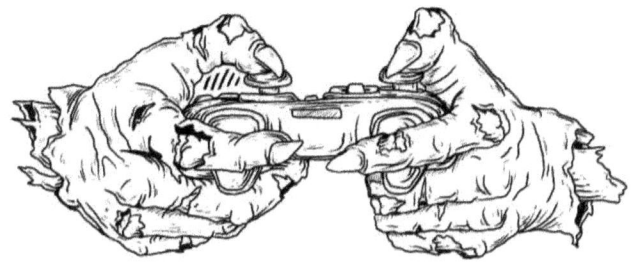

NOBODY

I wish I'd sink into my bed while I sleep.

Into an oblivion of perfect prosperity
Away from the devil's nest,
His people and their tendencies,
Into a world of colour and clarity,

Where life is monotonous yet interesting,
Not divided by this fanciful society.
Where you could live without a license,
Where you die for life with true essence,
Where you learn the doctrines of science,
Where you forget faith in these elusive beings,
Lies of a figmentary existence.

Here, love meets art and births life.
Here, you'd cry, scream, grieve, and laugh.
For what's the soul without burdensome strife?
Here, it isn't about rust, about treachery, about war,
It's about peace and love perfectly balanced on the edge of a knife.
I sink into a deeper space,

Umber Oblivion

Here, I live and love,
Here, I laugh and grieve
Here it isn't about anybody,
Here is an oblivion in me,
Here is nobody.

The asphalt got better with time, the buildings went from being five stories to 20 stories, the river ate the bank every monsoon, and the rains got weaker as the sun dried up this cemented giant. Surat, a city that grew up with me, I lived close to the river bank and watched the murky waters rise every now and then with admiration and curiosity. I remember running around the streets, and it showed me nothing but love. My city was quite small initially, maybe because I never had the courage to roam. It was the very first time that I stepped outside the boundary that I had created for myself during the 7th grade summer vacations, right after our exams.

Arihant, Dikshit, Goldy, Samyak, and Arin now Bobby, this prepubescent gang of children, gave me a gist of what Surat looked like up close. We jumped railings, took selfies, and ran around with our little feet. I never really cared about what the city looked like, but now that I have had a taste of it, I do not want to return. Initially, I roamed around in passenger cars. Since I was fun-sized, I usually sat with the driver, and that was the best seat one could get. I believe I travelled longer distances; I travelled further to the theatres, malls, turf, and other schools. When I was a teenager, I had access to a moped, and my boundaries disappeared. That was when Surat revealed itself to me; it reeked with malice, hate, and anger. Even though I was exposed to all of these before, it was now that I was experiencing them frequently. I explored every nook and cranny of the city. I chased sunsets and sunrises; even the scorching noon couldn't stop me. Then, when I ultimately fell in love with Surat, I got used to its breath, and as it got used to mine, I had to abandon her. I sometimes think that she knew me; she loved me too, and every now and then she looks for me, and I do too.

Chapter - 5
Nalla Kutty

My emotions were ignored and vandalized throughout my teenage years. I was around 13 years old when this boy named Deva came into our class. He was a Malayali, one of my own. He ridiculed my guts, and he always wondered why I was the way I was. He even shifted his class because I messed with him and cussed at him.

One fine day, I ran into Deva and his mom, and she asked me to walk with her. I walk along the path that leads us to the hospital canteen. She asked about my parents and my house, and I kept answering as I distracted myself from her questions, fidgeting around like a keyed toy. She bought me a plate of Manchurian and a drink and sat down with me and tried to reason why I was the way I was. She showed concern, and I felt good. Before she left, she said, "Nalla kutty aavanam." It had been a long time since anyone talked to me with sympathy or love. I nodded and ran back to the school. It was crazy how a little bit of love had been imprinted on my heart as a core memory.

Chapter - 6

Old Friend

"I gently pulled the mesh door to prevent it from making a noise when opened. I called him out and negotiated the possibility of him coming to hang out with me. Usually, he would refuse initially, but I wouldn't give up until one of his parents came out and denied it or if he agreed. He is one of the oldest friends I've ever had; we watched each other grow up. We were classmates, and even when I repeated grade 2, he didn't treat me differently. Maybe I was just too good a friend, or maybe he didn't think much of it. Anyway, Manish and I started exploring the internet during our pre-teen years. We would secretly watch things we shouldn't, but it had a rebellious adrenaline rush to it— it was fun. We thought we were ready for what the world had in store for us. We would text girls from each other's accounts, brainstorming what the next text should be. It was fun, new, and addictive because talking to people on the internet was strange but felt so good.

We grew up to be good friends, too. We would spend a lot of time together in church, game zones, on the ground—almost everywhere. But along the way, it all faded away. I don't really know when or why it happened, but it wasn't bad talking to him after almost a year; maybe all the awkwardness was in my head, or maybe it just wasn't there. I believe we all grow out of our differences, or time makes them vague, and every day you forget what really went wrong."

ABSCONDING SANITY

I linger in this loop of absconding reality.
For what's real is cursed since I've been birthed into this tragedy.
Each day begins with a wail and ends with a malady.
Transgression runs through our veins, for sins area rhapsody.

With blood, did we create a ripple?
Our eyes blinded our mouths muffled
The truth banished the lies tripled
Our tears vanished, and our voices crippled.
For we've lived in envy and died in hatred.
The people torment, yet again, love was forsaken.
We stood up on pillars of lies and prejudice.

In perfect harmony was pride awaken.

When we drench in this iniquitous rain
Do we relish this pain?
Do we exalt these slaughter stains?
But when you gently slither into your eyes
You realize you and I would never be sane.

Chapter - 7
Mirage

It was church day, and we came back in the afternoon after the morning service. We had a small group of friends, and we went around the hospital to pray for people. I wasn't really excited about this, but I liked meeting new people. If Mummy had been here, she'd be proud of me, but being away might've made her want me to do what I was doing. We'd go in together and pray for the sick, sing a couple of songs, and leave. Like any regular day, I walked into the church compound and was looking for people, and as I kept walking, I saw Mummy walking towards me. For a moment, everything around me disappeared. I froze and kept staring at her. I wanted to run right into her arms and tell her how much I missed her and that I wanted her to stay with us this time.

I kept walking, and as I did, my heart seemed to be heavier than before. I knew I'd feel better once she held me. I took a few more steps, and I realized it wasn't Mom; it was just someone who looked exactly like her—big eyes and curly hair. I would do anything in the world for that woman to be my mom, but she wasn't. I felt devastated knowing it wasn't her and disgusted thinking I couldn't recognize who Mummy was and who wasn't; it was the first time I realized I needed glasses. That little child did not cry; he was soon distracted by the chaos that he carried along with him, something that kept him from breaking. something more than just unceasing pain.

Mother Mirage

Certain junctures in life remind me how much
I need you.

I remember the time I let go of your finger.
I wandered into the crowd, not knowing where my little
feet would lead me.
Frantic, scared, and lost your hand, my eyes sought
I remember all through the chaos.

I wouldn't let go of that finger no more.
Someday, sometime, I wish you walk through that door.

I'd still be the boy I was.
Just bigger, petrified, lonely, and sore

I recall having my arms around a wraith.
Convincing myself it was you
Isn't all this an ugly gamble?

Love was to play you, and I were the bait.

I believe I will come to rest in your arms someday.
Living to shatter the mirage I created to fill the grey,
Hoping I'd still hold your finger.
Hoping to live that tomorrow, I rest today.

Mummy shifted when I was in 7th grade. I did not exactly understand the concept of it. We went to the airport to bid her goodbye, and as she left, I kept looking at a vulnerable woman who loved her kids yet wanted to move—a woman who left her 13-year-old behind. I looked at her as she vanished into the crowd. I went back to the car, and as everyone slept, I wept into my jacket. I wept until someone woke up; I'd instantly wipe the tears and rest as though nothing had happened.

I went back home and told all my friends that my mom had gone to the U.S. That evening, I came back home, took a nap, woke up, and started looking for my mother. As I glanced into the last room, hoping for my mom to be there, I knew in the back of my head that she wasn't home. I wished I could cry at that very moment, but I couldn't. I was just dismayed and shocked and had to convince myself to stop looking. I wish someone had been there to tell me everything would be alright, but I was only given sympathy when my family was the topic of discussion.

This eventually affected my poetry a lot. I don't know why every time I pick up a pen, everything that I write on paper turns out to be a descriptive painting of my thoughts. I have not been able to write anything happy as of yet, but I hope I can do it in the near future. The dark keeps me comfortable, keeps me poised and calm, and happiness intrigues me, yet it scares me. I'm scared it will all fade away in time. I'm scared that being happy brings sadness.

Amma

It's been six years and a million tears.
I miss the palm I held when
I walked through my fears. I wish I could run into your arms like I did.
I wish you were near.

You've made me who I am,
Even though you are a thousand miles away,
I'll still hold your hand as I sway.
In my heart, you'll always stay.

I'll cling onto the stories you told me.
You'll always be my warrior.
And I'll always be your little boy,
I promise to be the man I told you I'd be.
I promise I'll try.

Chapter – 8

Dopamine

The necessity of dopamine has invoked a belt of problems that go unnoticed and strangely. The rustling of leaves, the rumbling of the cold wind—all marked under obnoxiously loud people and their daily rambling about how taking part in this rat race makes sense. How much everything you lift is worth directly depends on the same abstract destiny one is supposed to reach. The very thought of it makes me disgusted. OH! How stories and tales were told stories of glory and greatness. OH! How all these stories were washed away in a wretched gutter.

There are times when I'm too exhausted when I lie down to my bed, resting try to while time away, but my head gives up, and I feel too tired to think about all the people that I picture. They turn into caricatures trapped in this part of my mind that won't come out. Now, this leaves me sleepless until I stare too long at the dark ceiling and the sound of the cricket fleeces my ear.

Now that I sit idle, trying to recall the happy things, I cannot find them in me, maybe because it's all clouded under the trauma, but that isn't the case, I now think. My brain just does not feel like feeling happy; it's hard for me to explain it, yet it is what it is. I could remember instances like when my mom returned and how excited I was to get presents from her. At that time, I wasn't that excited to see Mummy, but to see the things she got me, and now that these years have passed, I wish I had been a better son. I wish I could embrace her like I did when I was young.

When Mummy left, I was almost as tall as her, yet shorter than my father. Now that I haven't seen her for eight long years, I sometimes picture how she'd look next to me. All these years went by, and I grew a little too tall. I wouldn't be able to walk inside her, wrapping her legs, when I was scared. I wouldn't be able to sit on her lap as her curly hair poked my face. All those things would have changed, but one thing that remains constant is her being my mom.

We Incarcerate Life

Who smeared my veins with blood?

Why am I a mortal?
I am at ease as I gently dive into sleep.
For I rise, I hopelessly long for my life to take a leap.
Mortality and life you sowed; iniquity and malice you reap.

We created Gods and demons, sinners and healers.
Men preached love and created shackles.
They murdered and massacred over nickels,
For even Judas sacrificed the Almighty for 30 mere shingles.

For we are one yet different,
We've created these borders; we've created the fear that we render. Our tongue, our colour, our land, and the ones we remember
The crook is set free; we incarcerate the bystander.

We are born into sin.
In sin, we die.
Let's all witness promises that lie.
As we all grieve as life goes by.

Chapter - 9

Papa

Udayakumar, for the man whose identity I've borrowed, there have been times when I've despised my father, and I have no shame in acknowledging that fact. A broken marriage had taken a toll on him, and that affected us as a family, yet he's managed to be around just for the love he has for my brother and me. During my teenage years, I made a decision that I'd never have a marriage like that of my parents; I'd never want a partner like they chose each other. Then there's another part of me that knows I could never be the father he is; I could never parent a child like he's managed to. The sacrifices that he's made for the family are a testimony to a love that I've never understood. The ambitions that I have stemmed from my father, and the creativity that runs through my veins also stems from him. He made me the man I have managed to be, and I believe he's done an excellent job. I remember the first few months when Mummy left; it was hard for him to cook for us, be attentive to our academics, and still manage to work, yet he did it all without complaining. There have been times when I questioned his contribution to our family, and I will never really forgive myself for those things that I've said, but I believe I will at least try and love him the way he's loved us, Someday I'd be able to stand in front of him, look him in the eyes and hug him. I'd tell him that I am grateful and will always be grateful to him for teaching me how to dream. I'll rest on his shoulders acknowledging that he dreamt for me, even then I know that I will never in a thousand years be able to repay the things he's done for me, and for that, I carry around a little reflection of his face, his blood in my veins and his thoughts in my head.

Dreams And Tribulations

We all live a synchronized, synthesized lie.

From the stifled patter of those tiny feet,

To the very moment you die,
These factory institutions,
They kill skill-dyed brains; you realize when you look back and sigh.

Matrixed, marginalized, sick, sycophantic world,
We don't learn; we are impelled and taught.
We are all bred in a herd.

The ones who don't believe are asserted insane.
The rest call upon a covert Lord.
We all scoff at ways we do not believe.
How you live is something I do not perceive.
What you feel when all these fancied tribulations you heave,
You almost insignificantly comprehend what life is.
But then it's already time for you to leave.

We forget that life is living.
For we've forgotten to dream,
We've stuck ourselves to grieving,
For we all must go someday,
We might as well take the narrow way.

Chapter – 10
The Man In The Sky

Sometimes, I think a bit too much when I'm sad, and I just can't remember how much pain was inflicted on my younger self, yet I do know all that did happen. I knew the world would slap me around if I did not stand up for myself. It made me think I had to maintain a persona that surpassed bullies, especially the elders. These are the worst kind of people—the ones that call themselves the elders. They make assumptions, trigger your emotions, and leave you questioning things that you would've been fine with. I was truly saddened by the amount of humanity they are willing to sacrifice just to get tea from a 7-year-old boy. I was often asked about how things were at home; they'd be all ears at first and then let out an exaggerated sigh that was supposed to cure me from all the trauma that I had. The ones that leave me questioning why am I this troubled, I did believe that the man in the sky would help me through these tormenting times. I couldn't be more wrong. I just conversed with the wind through years of innocence, hoping and believing in a person who'd help me steer away from these redundant episodes of aggressive abhor. Each time that I knelt, I did feel that this would be the last, that this is how pain ends, yet I'd still be troubled with life just meddling with its horned forehead that smashes into the fine thread of happiness that I delicately create. I just watch as everything around me drags me into sharp gravel that scrapes my memories.

Sometimes, it's just clouded with a lot of ambiguity amongst anger, lust, desire, and exhaustion, and I like it there. Chaotic yet calming. The thoughts that I get some days are disturbing to the people around me when I narrate them to them. I've always thought of it as a perk of being different, yet it was more than that. It was more than just different; it was duplication, murder, multiplication, and everything that had blood in it. These thoughts scared me at first. I started distracting myself from it, trying not to be reminded of thoughts of blood and gore, but after a while, I gave in to it. This affected my poetry a lot. I don't know why every time I pick up a pen, everything that I write on paper turns out to be a descriptive painting of my thoughts. I have not been able to write anything happy as of yet, but I hope I can do it in the near future. The dark keeps me comfortable, keeps me poised and calm, and happiness intrigues me, yet it scares me. I'm scared it will all fade away in time. I'm scared that being happy brings sadness.

Ichor Slaves

I see a man devour an angel.

The feathers turned grim, and its eyes grew stranger.
Men rejoiced while blood flooded the manger.

Ichor filled the air the mongrels whine as they
smelt danger.

I walked through thistles and thorns.
Salvation, Salvation! for heaven they mourn

I see no man above the sky. I see no golden lawn.
Massacre and treachery through the night
God and gospel through the dawn.

We are slaves to ourselves.
We poison our rivers.
While we stare at our empty wells.
For one remains famished and hungered, and the
other swells.

Umber Oblivion

I scoff at your hypocrisy.
I live for no man, no god.
Dub me insane.
For I perceive no Alpha no Omega
Where is your almighty Lord?

I live yet another day.
On this thin thread of life and death, I sway
Go look at yourself and ask
To whom do I pray?

Plaster Saint

You rip out each asbestos from my weak,
Dangling house, pulling me down while this whole world
looks upon me,

With an eerie, wicked frown,
Mocking men who despise the ways of this fanciful
society,
Torment them, dub them clowns,

You and your plaster saint rule,
Those that forsake them labelled fools,
Foraging a child's dreams while he drools
You manufacture a definite genus of fools.

We are bred in the hope of survival.
While our ways are profane and trivial,
You and I are bred into a herd.
Forget being an individual.

Let's cling to what we are taught.
While our blood agglutinates with this society
and clots,
Let's live in the hope of telling stories that we lived,
We hoped that we fought.

Iscariot Judas

What would it be like to dangle from a
hangman's noose?

Would it suffice my thirst for peace?
Would it rend to my pain?
Or would it just be agony's unending ruse?
For when I gently flutter on the knot,
I hitch. I fall into an oblivion, a ghastly ditch.
Where did I learn what life had been?

Where I see what my orb hadn't seen?
Maybe this was what I existed for.
This nihilistic moment,
I put down the weight of the reality I bore.
Yet when all of life I tore
I still stumble into torment, misery, and sore
Would I rest my chin on a knot someday?
Would I still be loved as I am today?
Should I wait till carnage gets through us?
Or would I just be this world's Iscariot Judas?

DUBIOUS PSALM

For when I knock the gates of heaven,
would you let me in?

Or would you persecute me for being human?
Mankind is flawed and treacherous.
Am I to blame? I was given this mortal rumen.

Why make the gates of heaven golden?
While you create cannibalistic men who fight
for fodder,
For one has tomes, and the other rocks on
his shoulder.
For one rests under a mansion; the other croaks as it
gets colder.

You claim to be the Alpha, the Omega, the beginning,
and the end.
For millions of us, rest upon hopelessness
We called upon you, destitute and dejected.
Whose life did you mend?
For I am mortal, for I am man
Tomorrow, I could be dirt or a leper.
But before I depart, tell me
My Lord, are you, my shepherd?

Chapter - 11
Adrenaline Hunger

The pre-teen years of my life were quite interesting. This was when I first started to feel things. I was scared of hate, adrenaline, lust, anger, and extreme amounts of underlying energy that were suppressed under the tight school tie around my neck. I started to explore, and it was quite hard for me to navigate through rights and wrongs. I started to think about violence a lot, maybe because it wasn't let out when I was a child, but that is no reason to think of slapping people in the face while they were conversing; I never really got myself to do it. I've pictured it a million times, like a fantasy that sticks to you through puberty, but it never plays out. Maybe I wasn't ready for the consequences, or maybe I just couldn't, but I believe that in that very moment when my hands fell across her, there was some sort of realization that reminded me that I'm a human, and humans do not behave that way.

The jokes around me started getting more sexual, more personal, and more humorous, according to the pre-teen Romil. We would joke about every last thing we should've empathized with; we laughed and we cried, and yet all of it seems so hazy that it makes me want to lie down in a fetal position and launch myself into a long-forgotten yesterday. I sometimes wish I could crawl into people's heads to glance at their favorite memories so that I could feel the pain a little more when I am reminiscent of the happiness that has long gone. This was when I started to drift off religion, not because I wasn't taught enough but because I grew up. I started to get curious about how things worked and wasn't happy with answers with no real possibility of discovery. Everything seemed so complicated yet easily explained. I respect the way I was brought up. Religion gave me ethics, but I couldn't find a God.

As I grew up, I walked out into the darkness for answers, yet I believe I haven't found them yet. Along the way towards answers, intervals of light shine through a small peep from the shell built around me, guiding me to take a path I was not supposed to, otherwise. I lived a life of escapism, especially around that age, because every other thing that I went to was a distraction. I sometimes walked to the playground sobbing and bawling for something silly, yet I knew all of it would be gone if I stepped on for a game or saw some of my friends.

THE SUN MADE LOVE

I glance at what I was and envy I saw,

The sun makes love to the sky.
The sky then blushed a seraphic color
Aerating in this eerie act called love, it worships and rejoices in something so malicious. It revealed that it has fallen in love over something so vicious.

I then gently die under the blush sky.
Waiting to leave this mortal self, screeching a yonder sigh,
A divine creature then drops down with wings like that of a vulture.
It claws into my chest and augments onto my corse.

As my soul swims away into a hill, My corse romanticizes this earth.
It makes love with the petrichor.
Sacrificing itself for dust,
A divine inclusion I fulfill, morality.

I am drunk in the sunshine,
Lingering along instances of insanity
I try and rest on a mountain peak.
Yet when I blink again,
I were crucified on the vulture's beak.

Gallows Of Love

I've been captured and chained.

My wrists soak in blood,
Yet my heart grew numb; it felt no pain.
I looked up and smiled one last time as my soul gently drained.
I've got a billion questions that still agonize me.
For it was a legion of hate and pain that raised me.

My little self was in search of affection.
Uncertain of the ways it sluggishly erased me.
Is grave the path to peace?
Will my torment be at ease?
Will my nightmares cease? Promise me love,
With a wreathen dagger, my veins I'd crease.
I still live to die someday.
I still love it; afraid it would fade away.
I still sob, yearning to find a way.
For I was cursed to be a mortal, to be lost, to be a stray.

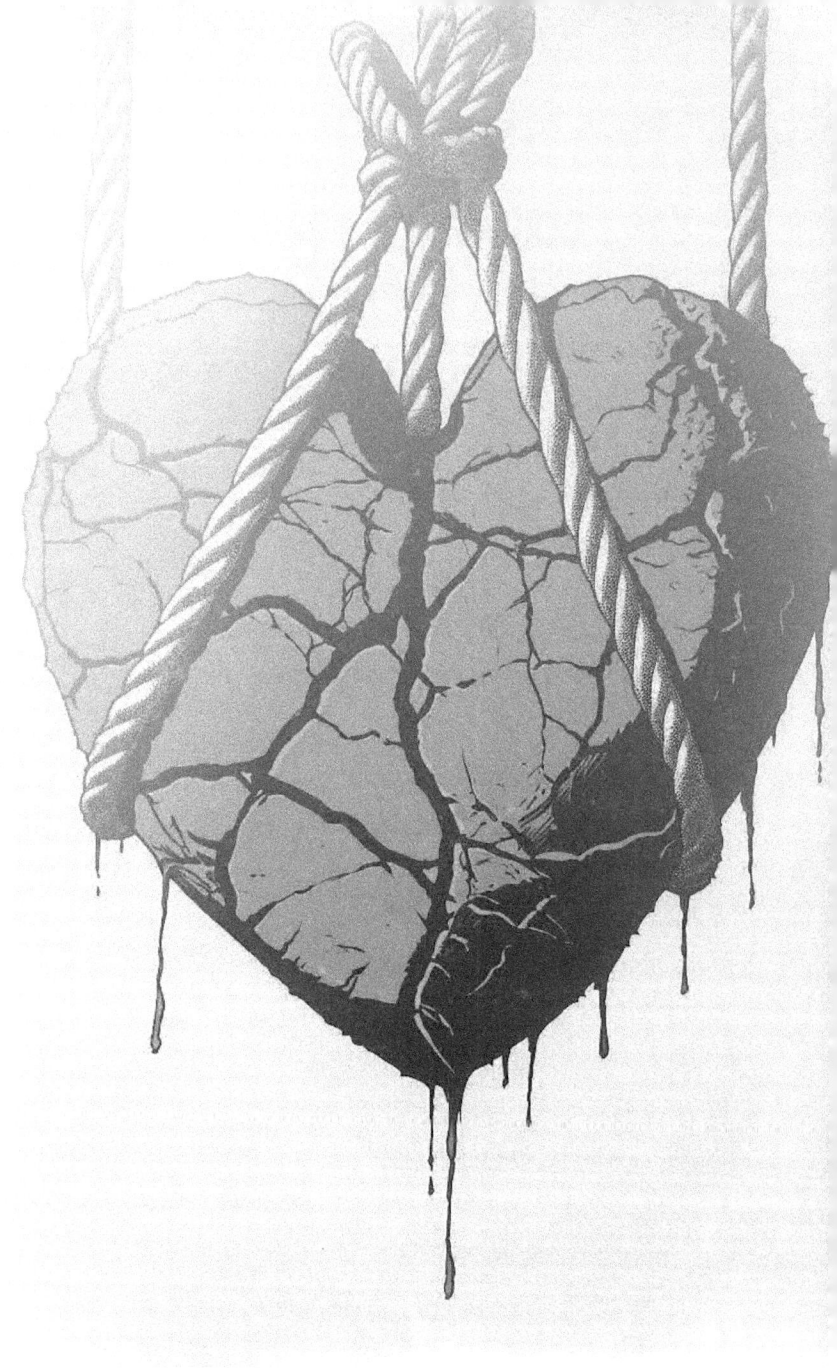

Even though I am in love with the idea of escapism, I think I would never be capable of it, not because there are no means to it but because there are ties and responsibilities I enjoy. These small moments of joy that sneak in via responsibilities and ties contribute heavily to the life that I am living, and they make a gigantic difference in my chaotic life. I have no doubts about how these moments turn hostile and aggressive during times of agony when each and every question opens us up to more vulnerability. Am I supposed to feel joy? Was it real? When will it return? When I am riddled with questions as such, I try to stick to the possibility of tomorrow. A tomorrow unworthy of life. Yet as life pierces through it, these questions tend to be feeble. The promises turn brittle, yet all of it seems so promising.

Now that I know there is no escapism, it does not make a difference in my life; it makes me who I was supposed to be rather than who I chose to become. I will loathe these detrimental moments, not because I deserve them but because they are proof of my mortality. While I try to answer these questions, I might as well try to live a little. For when this mortal planet dies and returns to dust, I'll still have it in my soul. I'll still have minute reflections of the world I created around me. I despise this life an awful lot, but I wouldn't trade it for anything different.

Chapter - 12
Walk Way

Aniket, our friendship was so passionate that we'd go to war for each other at any point in time. I remember people telling me that he defended me when he should've just kept silent, and I don't know, nobody's ever done that for me, and I did not realize how important that friendship was for me. Gradually, as time passed, we grew distant, or I grew distant. I knew what was happening, yet I just did not react to the situation. He was the first name I thought of when I thought about friends, but then I gave that outcome a second thought. Things got so bad between us that we almost fought and wouldn't talk without a mediator. I kept remembering all the things he'd done for me, yet I couldn't tame my ego to confront the problem. I sometimes sit around and look at things that remind me of his friendship. When I see anything that closely relates to. Superman, I remember him gifting me this candy vending toy that he got for me; it was cool, and I remember gifting him this chocolate bar that said, "I love you to the moon and back." That friendship had been buried long ago. Now that almost 3 years have passed, we've grown into our respective lives, still oblivious to the fact that a young friendship has died.

Divyanshu and I were like the duo everyone knew would be around together. There had been times when we acted like the latter never existed, but soon enough, we'd find reasons to hang out. He was this quiet dude who never really talked to anybody, but if you got to know him, the whole perspective of who he is changed. I've had the happiest, most adrenaline-pumping moments of my life with him. I remember him, Sulaim, and I sitting under the bridge, which was off-limits for us students, but to while away our time looking at the river talking, cussing, wrestling, and whatnot, we'd go there without fail. That fine day, I returned from Kerala, and he was the first person I met. We sat under the bridge like always and talked about random things that intrigued us. We were watching the new Justice League trailer, the Snyder Cut, and that's when Divyanshu said, "Bhai we've never been caught. I guess we should name this place or something". After that very moment, a constable walked to us and started frisking us and asking questions. But we stood our ground. Later, he said he'd take us to the inspector; I did not know why. I glanced while following the policeman, and that's when Divyanshu signaled me to run. I ran, and they followed. We ran in such a way that the others sitting under the bridge started running with us. After around 500 meters of non - stop running, we looked behind and simultaneously let out a sigh of relief, which quickly vanished when we saw the policeman chasing us on a moped. We immediately scaled the garden and started running on the walkway that was created near the riverbank. We ran for a while and heard a faint cry. Our friend was caught, and while he was there toiling, we kept running. We knew we'd be manhandled if we were caught. After keeping a safe distance, we hitched a ride to the school, where we sent our friends to vouch for Sulaim, who was caught. Well, I'm happy that things ended happily.

Time Lives

I relentlessly try to jot the stars that I dream about.

While the glitter on it vitiates and starts to rot,
When the gleam on it begins to scar,
I look up into the murky sky and wonder how I've come this far.

The streets I've walked through mock life,
Yet it rejoices when friction runs through;
it rejoices human strife,
These noises, these colors my dreams, they bribe,
The dark does not help no more.
I've been lost trying to hide.

I walk through valleys and gallows.
I run from grief and shadows.
For my heart lives, yet it feels so hollow.
I still hold on to the time I borrow.

Will this grief prevail forever?
Will these stars stay together?
For time massacres the omnipotent,
For time lives forever.

It was a moderately cold winter evening. I had no family in town; it wasn't a new feeling, but I believe everybody needs somebody at a certain point in time. The winter had just begun, and I piled myself with a lot of work. I had to dress up. I had to do my hair well. It hadn't been a problem, but ever since the ends started curling, I looked informal, as they say. Everything had become incoherent to me, and I did not know where I'd start. So, the best decision I could make was to sit and think about it, and that's when Jenis and Vraj told me they'd take me to the barber. I sat there, hoping the barber would style it like I wanted, but he did not. That's when Jenis took over. I sat there thinking about how I'd perform later that night, and the next stop was home. Both of them dressed me and told me I was handsome. I couldn't savor that moment because I was hasty, but that feeling was the closest thing to family; that very feeling was love.

I Yearn To Live

I don't believe in going to a place I've never been.

For when I'd be no more,
I'd walk through paths I've never seen,
I'd befriend beasts and spooks.
For this is home: the blue, the brown, and the green.

I'd touch the sky and glide down.
Here, I see nobody grieve, whine, or frown.
Peace resides in places with no disparity.
Here's no suffering.
No shame, no lord, no crown.

There's more to this life,
More than survival, more than strife,
More than murder, more than war,
For love, truth, and hope aren't too far.

I yearn to live and die for love.
I yearn to live for broken promises.
I yearn to live for friendship.
I yearn to live.

Chapter – 13

Ocean Eyes

At times, I find myself desolate and thirsty for that deific feeling that once took over my thoughts. I wish it had stayed like misery does, but that's just something about love; you wouldn't get a shred of it when you needed it the most. I have often failed to recognize love; I have failed to love like I have been loved, but what excites me is that this feeling never really leaves you; it just conceals itself for a while, maybe because no human deserves continuous love or maybe because we'd fail to savor it. Whatever the cause is, I know I live a little more when I fall in love, when I've been loved, and when I love. This is why I write poems of love: to divulge something that I would rather not if my loved one were right in front of me. Imbibing love out of experiences, I create poetry.

The closest I've been to love is in nuances I could never elucidate, that hazy memory of me walking around the market with my mum's shawl in my hand, I couldn't be safer. I kept walking along her shadow, hoping to find a vegetable that looked like an animal, and there it was, the perfect tomato that looked like the sparrow that flew by my window, my eyes had to admire the beauty of that vegetable or fruit as people claim, that admiration would not last long. For a moment I couldn't feel the pull- on mums' shawl that's when everything around me suddenly turned terrifying I gazed into every corner my eyes could reach but my thoughts blurred in the bangarang of the market all I could think of was me being abducted and that's when I broke I started bawling like any child who got lost in a crowded market would. That was one of the scariest moments of my childhood. It would seem like an exaggeration, but try explaining that to an eight-year-old. I started tiptoeing hesitantly in a direction I thought would be accurate, still having my face drenched in tears and mucus. That's when I felt a touch on my shoulder, and little me just knew that it was mummy; that very nuance was love.

Paradise I Have Found

You are elixir to a wandering traveller.
I'd delineate thousand tales of your beauty.
For I feel anchored and firm when life's been drifty.
A distinctive being, as if love fulfilled its duty.

She felt like a dreamy sunset.
Over a beautiful flower bed
A thousand stories of happiness,
I've read a seraphic path to paradise it led.

For when a man meets love like this
He craves to live in this paradise bliss.
For I'd live like this a thousand years.
I'd love like this a thousand years.

Shallow Star

I'm like the clingy chunk of tobacco on your half-smoked cigarette.

I find it hard to let go.
Life puts me in shallow waters, yet with all my might,
I row.
Oblivious of the consequence in these salty waters,
I sow.

I glare into the mirror; its not me I see.
Its someone I used to be.
For when the world ceases to breathe
With you, I'd be
For its you and me, I'd like to see.

Would you remember the days I curled up under your arms?
Would you remember me through these hollow nights?
Would you remember you've held my hand and whispered, "Darling, it's all gon be alright?"
For this world seems so desolate without you is a cursed sight.

Umber Oblivion

I still look for you in these stars.
I still look for you in these scars.
For you've been a part of what I am
For it's just us; I know everything else is a sham.

We found a bench right in front of a river that stood still. It mimicked the exact feeling I had in my heart. I was seventeen and had no idea where life was taking me. I just decided to stay still while it did. I had nothing to myself but my thoughts and a mesmerizingly beautiful girl we'll call Jinx. She sat right beside me. Maybe because we shared each other's melancholy, she took part in my solitary. We sat there, hovering our eyes over everything a teenager would find amusing, imagining how the river would look if we constructed a Ferris wheel in the water, which submerged into the murky river and took us back up. She even sketched it so that we give birth to an infinite memory, as she says. That feeling was home; the reality we created around us to escape what tormented us was love.

As it breaks my heart to narrate an experience I try not to be reminded of, I walk back into the same streets of joy when I've dreaded the reality around me. Certain music, certain smells Certain phrases remind me of Jinx at times. I decided to watch this movie called Stand by Me, and there was this music that she had as her ringtone. I sat there on the couch staring at the TV, but my mind soared through the streets that lay along the school, us walking around the same path a million times and still not getting tired of it, those streets that have eavesdropped on every lover that our school gave birth to. I was a teenager under the street light, knowing no bounds of joy when she said she'd be my muse. I danced and I sang. I embraced her as much as I could, and yet all of it slipped off my fingertips like a handful of sand being drowned in the ocean. This reminiscence reminds me of all the things that I chose to be and how I loved being who I was—never really concrete on ideas but always distracted with absurd ideas and a smart mouth. I never really thought people would like listening to me until I met her; I was lucky she did. It was indeed difficult to move away from someone you shared dreams with. I reached Kerala in absolutely no anticipation. I had zero hopes of surviving here. I pulled myself together with a thin thread of endless conversations and dreams of getting to meet her. Yet it all died when it was fated to.

An Eternal Mortal

Is this life enough, or would I need a thousand
more? I've fallen in those ocean eyes,
Gently drifting away to an oblivious horizon,
Hoping to find love, hoping to find a shore.

But when I walk among these trees,
When I caress these flowers,
I wish I had your hand to hold.
I wish for warmth in the cold.

You make me feel eternal.
I am earthly yet a blessed mortal.
For I got to relish love's deific morsel,
Therefore, I'll live, I will be immortal.

For when I've done my time here,
And my heart halts,
I'll make myself a paradise,
I yearn to be infinitely lost in those ocean eyes.

WOULD YOU TOO

The shirt you gave me don't smell like you no more,
Am I in love, or am I just sore?
You make me feel eternal, two souls and one heart we bore.

I still stare at the door, hoping for you to come through.
I still look at the sky, and its colors remind me of you.
And just when the sun sets and the orange washes away in the blue,
I look at the night sky, hoping for my wishes to come true.

I'd walk through conversations we've had,
I feel happy that I have you, but the distance makes me sad.
You are the bright summer and the cozy winter,
You've walked me through storms, and if you let go, what would I have had?

I hope you still smile at the sun like I do.
I hope you still walk through the rain like I do
I hope you look at the night sky like I do.
I hope, I love, and I live
Would you too, like I do?

I've never met someone as broken as her. In complete misery, but her eyes sparkle as she talks about her past, and even though I knew all of it, I managed to break her a little more. The patience some people show because of admiration and love is impeccable. It's almost superhuman to love without conditions and to love someone who pushes you away. I knew about the love she had for me; I knew she would prove it over and over again if she had to.

I looked at her to get answers to my 'why,' but she didn't have any. She mumbled things because she felt like she'd make sense, but she did not. That, to me, is sacrificial – to have broken wings but still lend feathers from your back to the person you love. That's what I feel when I am beside her. I cannot thank her enough for carrying around this weight of mine that I sometimes lay on her. It isn't gratitude that I have for her; it isn't thankfulness. It is pride and admiration I have for the woman she is and for the love she has
for me.

I remember being bullied by a bunch of seniors the first week I attended college. I remember having my friends around me, but none of them reacted. But as those guys held my collar and threatened me, I remember having her beside me, defending me. That, to me, is strength. Her urge to fight for me is absolutely unimaginable, and I believe she would wage a war against the world for me. It seems like an exaggeration, but isn't all of life an exaggeration of mild feelings and thoughts overwhelmingly baiting us into reactions? And I gladly give in to this bait called love.

I might sound touchy or a little too personal, but to be in love is one of the best feelings one could ever experience. It isn't heavenly or divine; it's as human as it could be. And that makes it special; that makes it worth living. Therefore, to drown in her love, I live. And someday, as the sun sets on me, I hope I rest on her lap as she caresses this flawed heart of mine."

Chapter – 14
Merry Christmas

Noel was born on Christmas Day; his birthday was considered special. As a boy, I was pretty jealous of the fact that he had double special treatment. Even though I wanted to have a birthday as special as Christmas, all I had was two days after Independence Day. I'd have to find ways to stay relevant that day; everything was about him. We stayed up that night, we sang Christmas carols, and he dressed up as Santa. Well, that time had passed in an instant. I was this big boy living all by himself. I soon turned into a lonely teenager in a city full of people I knew, yet nobody felt like home. I was alone in a flat that Aayush and I rented out, or Golden Park, as it was called. It did give me a lot of bittersweet memories. It was Christmas day; I had no family in town, and that was the first time I had to live through Christmas without my family. There were no carol songs, there was no church I wanted to visit. I enjoyed loathing in misery, but I still wanted my family around. Those 24 hours were slow. I was jealous at times. I did want a bit of the attention that Noel got, but that day, I just wanted him to be around.

Vain Eternity

I poison myself every now and then to stimulate the numb in me

I bow unto the shackles of abhor.
I stray into the shallow, drown in ignominy.
Degenerating and dwindling with time.
I forget who I was.
I forget what's mine.
Yet again, I will walk the lonely road.
Yet again, will I slug the moonshine?
Will I mimic the nightmares that my iris holds?
Will I shimmer in the face of agony?
Will I bleed in gold?
Will I retch in disgrace and tragedy?
Will I sink in hate?
Will my love turn cold?
In an eternity, will I know?
An eternity of dirt and life
An eternity of lust and shame
An eternity of happy pain
An eternity went vain.

Chapter - 15
Gaia

Through time, I've learned to be receptive to greater powers that I perceive—the waves, the petrichor, the trees, and the hills. They all define the feebleness of humans. Now that I've realized that they aren't here to mimic a God, but rather to help us think and admire their unending, ever-changing beauty. I understand that I am nothing but human.

Even though I am composed of the same elemental building blocks, I possess the ability to dream, to walk, to traverse the sky above, and to drink from the oceans below. I can close my eyelids and create an entirely different universe populated by feeble god-like beings. However, when I open my eyes, I am confronted with my human self, perpetually attempting to rewrite the story in which I exist. I can spend hours basking in the sunset's glow, only to be accompanied by a legion of thoughts that ravage what remains of me once darkness overtakes the horizon.

I sometimes want to stare into the sun, hoping it will burn my iris, killing away its gift of sight. I would then etch in the darkness tales I've never told before; I would run endlessly in the abyss that was burned into me; I would tumble upon death yet be unaware of it. I would live a thousand lives, each day a new tale, forgetting what the world looked like.

Would that be the bliss I've wanted?

I shunned enjoying the colors, now that I realize they've all been buried in my socket. Would I still think the way I do, or would it distort the color of my thoughts? I could be suspicious of every last thing that comes my way. I would be scared of the wind, the rain, the dirt, and the clay. I would live in my head a little more. A place that I dreaded, eventually trying to find a home in a strange land.

The house that I built crumbles into pieces as the smoke blows out, and the people of the land let out a jarring roar. Outnumbered, bruised, and calloused, I try to recall what life looked like, but I have been banished from seeing the life I led. I stand upon the hill of sin and wait for the clouds to bestow the sun's glory.

I strive to fulfill the quest of life that I conjure within my mind, traversing along desolate roads that were once brimming with life but are now suffocated under layers of asphalt. I yearn to construct the perfect paradise under which I could live, yet with each carefully placed piece, it seems to manifest into a hellish tragedy in which I am destined to reside.

Umber Oblivion

We Are Dirt

I love how the greens sing me a song every time I'm sore.

How I walk out my door to find the sky drenched in orange,
Yet each time I take a glance, I find more.
You'd never know what Gaia has in store.

I remember how you made me puddles of rain.
How my boat gently vanished down the drain.
Remember how you caressed my mane.
And yet, for everything you've done,
We've only driven you insane.

I remember the starry nights
I remember the cold loo,
I remember the storms,
I remember the floods,
I remember the rain and the flashy lights.

I still cherish every moment I walk through dirt
For thistles, thorns, flowers, and the petrichor,
Reminds me of who I am,
I am who you are,
I am dirt.

Chapter – 16
Snap Back To Reality

As each day passes, I wander in search of joy, happiness, and pleasure, but all of those things go by so quickly that within a snap, I'm back to where I was in complete agony. I sit on a tattered boat to sail through a deep, violent river, yet there are moments when sunlight strikes my gale and I feel alive again, and the moment I rub my eyes to embrace the joy, I drown myself in the loathing pain and momentous bullshit that life gives me. We care a little too much about each other's lives when every day we wake up to get a sneak peek into the lives of our adored humans. It begins when we watch and steal a memory's visual, just to watch it again and think that we'd feel the same way. We need to learn that our memories are not infinite. I almost feel like a technological laggard, but we need to stop forcing ourselves to mimic a life we expect to have. We need to stop consuming the ecstasy that self-importance gives us. Yet, what hurts me the most is that I write this on a laptop. I could've done it in a field under the sunset, basking in Gaia's beauty. But no, I'd rather sit inside concrete walls and stare at something as feebly interesting as a fan.

Umber Oblivion

Now that I realize I am a drowning preacher, I still urge you to live a little more. Stop trying to chain your memories from the best angle. Get closer to what life provides, feel every second of it, and just when you get to relish it, it vanishes into an oblivion of misery-filled nostalgia. My teenage years came at me quite unexpectedly. I let go of the self that I was and turned into this arrogant lad who had no concern about how others felt. I sometimes felt like I should've been hugged a bit more instead of being slapped, and yet I could change nothing but quiver when I was conditioned to be manhandled when things went wrong.

Quietus Reality

We are corpses scrambling around this forbidden land.

Marching away to the tunes of a quietus band,
On towers of iniquity, sin, and murder we stand,
Waiting to devour each other as everything sinks back into the sand.

The truth we believe in is a mirage of our perception.
If you look closer, it's all dust and deception.

Am I real, or am I just a figment of your delusion?

For everything I touch, everything I see feels like a hallucination.
I don't feel human no more.
I don't know me no more.
I feel empty and hollow.
Imprisoned in an ocean of sin so shallow.

But I believe
Beneath these covers of flesh lies a soul.
Beneath the dust and sham lies the truth.

Beneath your burdens lie dreams.
Dreams that reciprocate sanity,
Dreams that fabricate tomorrow's reality.

Acceptance of reality seems like a curse that runs you down and stabs you in the back of the neck, a place where you constantly fail to reach and pull the dagger out. As time passes, the dagger becomes a part of you and turns into the very lifeblood of your reality.

I fail to accept lies that propagate reality as a sham. I once read a quote that I vaguely remember: "Art and passion become a chore when you have to do them frequently." Therefore, it loses the very essence of passion and adopts monotony into itself, finally burying mediocrity in its chest. Even though I realize this is the truth, I constantly try and convince myself to love it in such depth that there is no monotony and that art has its passion.

I live to witness a day that has no friction with its time when intoxication seems unnecessary and life is the ichor to your divine world that births itself through the reality that you try to break. Until then, I will strive to witness that reverie that lives in my head. I linger in hope, rejoicing as it advances towards my future.

Divine Futility

We're intertwined in futile attempts to achieve serrated glory.
Pillars of dust and sham we birth to create a bed time story.
Under these stories are corpse of children, men, and women.
Buried under sin and tragedy, a vile sanctuary.

Human lives butchered and slain.
Your prestige you create stomping over corse in a fetid drain.
Our blood-stained hands we scoured with the divine rain.
Yet with all that we earn, this dirt inhumes our blood stain.

Humans don't deserve heaven.
Humans don't deserve a second chance.
Humans live for sin and pleasure.
Yet, all this could be a hallucination, a divine trance.

Celestial Slumber

Sometimes, I want to feel how the sun feels.

Glorious and alluring, yet suppressing the power to create life,
Strolling through paths unknown, sometimes into the night sky, I dive,
Swimming through the gates of heaven, inebriated by the ichor hive.
My wings of glory have clipped,
My dreams and stories have been ripped.
For the heavens I've visited have been shut,
The stars grieved, and the moon eclipsed.
The colors I have vitiates and rots,
The music I listen to corrodes and clots.
I created a labyrinthine of grief and torment.
Yet when in pain, I sought.

Would I ever taste the glory of a thousand stars?
Would I ever bathe in streams of elixir?
Would I paddle down the clouds of heaven?
Arcane worlds would I unravel?
Hoping someday sometime I would, I let go of this sphere, and I slither into the gravel.

Chapter – 17

Even Tide

The most admirable piece of art is the sunset. A poem that changes its color each day. Surat has the most beautiful sunsets. Ones that made me pause, ones that left me hanging for more. The ones that bind everything around it golden with their rays. The ones that made the sky a canvas of numerous works of art. The walkway and riverbank had the best view of the sunset, staring right at the sun as it gently withdrew itself into the horizon that swallowed it. Some sunsets deserved mere leave, and we deserved mere of these sunsets.

I sometimes wonder how life brought me to a place I don't like one bit. I understand how the people around me don't wish good for me and how they celebrate in my failure. Or maybe all of this is a sheath of lies that I create to satisfy my narcissism. As each day passes, I wander in search of joy, happiness, and pleasure, but all of those things go by so quickly that within a snap, I'm back to where I was in complete agony. I sit on a tattered board to sail through a deep, violent river, yet there are moments when sunlight strikes my gale, and I feel alive again and the moment. I rub my eyes to embrace the joy, I drown myself in the loathing pain and momentous bullshit that life gives me.

THe creation of My utopia

The soil soaked as the heavens wept.

A ladybug sought shelter on my palm.
I sat there in adoration; my eyes stood still.
The wind halted, and my heart grew calm
If only you could see the colors I saw,
Through tides and hills,
Evading jaws and claw,
For my dreams create no boundaries knows no law.
I held my masts up high.
Could listen to the waves roar and sigh,
Soon in the dark mountains I abode,
Drank from the river wild horses I rode.
All these must be just tall tales of fantasy.
Yet these tales keep me alive.
For when the world tries me and I rest my eyes,
Into my own little paradise, I dive.

Hark Ye

We abide in concrete towers built upon dead people,
The rich prevail while they bury the feeble.
For when the sky hurls hails of man-made fire,
The grim wails of infants suffuse an hour so dire.

When life walks through this boneyard yet again,
Will she feel the voices calling out his name?
Will she tremble listening to the muffled cries?
Will she feel the tremor of their eternal pain?

While you reside safely under his wing,
They recite the death knell's hymn,
While we gather around and sing,
Life brings them down to a murderous rim.

They look for a saviour.
They look for hope.
With eyes shut and hands tied,
The world hands them a rope.

Chapter - 18
Homeless

I hadn't gotten out of the house in 15 days when the lockdown started. It affected me a lot. My whole life was outside of my room; I never really spent time with myself, and slowly, I had forgotten to be alone. I met my friends after a fortnight. I did miss them, but more than that, I missed myself or who I was when I was with them. I came back home. My father knocks at my door and asks me to start packing. I saw fear in his eyes. He had a feeling we wouldn't survive the virus. I waited for him to leave my room, and then I started bawling my eyes out. I was shocked, but I mustered up the courage to ask him why we were leaving. After I was startled by that very statement, he looked at me and said, well, because there's nothing left here. I just looked at him and nodded. Everything I knew was in this city. Surat was home, yet I had to leave. I had to leave the place that had made me who I am. I rang up my friends and told them I'd be gone in three days. I did not get the time to take a last look at the places or the faces I loved. They got me cake, a farewell that I did not deserve. I was very happy as the adrenaline took over me, but eventually, I started to feel hollow. I knew that a significant part of me was being amputated.

Nihilistic Love

Sometimes, I feel like stabbing myself in the head.

To feel how my eyes would react to the gore limping
down my face, the warm blood imitating life.
Swallowing sweat and spit, augmenting to win the race.

My eyes seem sedately excited.
With gore, I etch my fate.
I wasn't lost in an ocean no more.
For it clot, shore did I create.

My eyes ran out of sight.
Was slinking into a stygian
And when I gently drain out of life
None was unveiled; it was all labyrinthine.
I haul the dagger out and walk into the mob again.
I linger for the deific rain.
Shackled in love and shriveled in odium
I walk into this nihilistic pain again.

Chapter - 19
Strange But Home

I went out for a ride with Anish and Richie. We roamed around the city and sat in the parking lot near Richie's place. That was when I felt this weight right around my chest, realizing that, just like the ride, my trip back home to Surat had come to an end. It was so painful. I looked at them and ranted out about everything that troubled me. I don't know if they were concerned, bored, or sleepy, but I'm happy that they were there. They sat there, listening to me spew out all kinds of curses against people I despise and every minute detail that frustrated me at that moment. I felt better; I felt like I could leave the place. I felt like I carried a lot of weight around, and they helped me put it down again. I still remember Anish's concerned face that remained unfazed even though my monologue went on for about two hours. Finally, he said, "We're here," and that phrase was enough to calm me down, to let me know that I was fine. Therefore, I've learned to be in the company of people who hold you when you need to be held, and sometimes, all you need is a pat on the back and a phrase of assurance.

RUGGED DREAMS

I gently stare into a blank space as life drifts off of my fist.

Oblivious of what I'll see, oblivious of where I'll be,
I walk through the city mist.
I run through thistles and thorns;
I've fallen a million times.
Oblivious of the times dirt I've kissed.

I wake up yet again to another day of nothingness.
I wake up to life, and yet I feel closer to death,
I wake up to the sun shining, the birds singing.
Yet, I think about what life would be like when I draw my last breath.

I fear life hasn't given much to me.
I fear what it has would all be taken away one day.
On this thin thread of possibilities, I sway,
I still yearn to live another day.

For what I was am not tomorrow,
For what is life without grief, death, and sorrow?

Umber Oblivion

For I choose to be who I am.
Yet when I choose not to,
I will still wake up tomorrow.

Yesterday, I noticed a picture of mine in a friend's wallet. I did not really know how it ended up there but the first thought that went across my head was, damn that is gay! I did not want to accept affection as a reason at that time, maybe because I was too hardened by the masculine sheath I constantly covered myself with.

Also, I was happy and overwhelmed. I couldn't help but shed a tear I looked at it for a while and acknowledged his love for me and returned it to him without mentioning a word; I just kept basking in that affection. I wanted to ask him about it, but it would've ruined the moment for me. Maybe because I couldn't really comprehend the idea of someone carrying around a picture of mine and that, too, a friend. I realize friends aren't just symbiotic beings that we inevitably have to live with; they're beings with whom we feel things, those that are more than just momentary pleasure.

To the symbiotic beings around you, acknowledge them, and let them know you love them. Maybe love has been a long gone feeling, and yet it does not take much time to return.

That is why we all deserve a little bit of love that sometimes surprises and overwhelms us with its fragility and genuineness. I could never really have predicted that moment that I now cherish forever.

Chapter – 20
Homeland

I moved to Kerala, and everything that I had suddenly left me. I found myself alone, hoping everything would be alright, hoping things would get better, but they did not seem to budge. I enrolled myself in college, hoping things would change, but I never really got out of the bubble that I had created for myself. I had just begun making friends, and it did not turn out well. The ones with whom I talked least in the first few months of my bachelor's degree became my friends. Febi, Amal, and Gokul were the friends I got when I wasn't looking for friends at all. They shared the same excitement I had when I spotted a pond and wondered what it would be like to swim in it, and that was it. We hung out at the pond, swam, wrestled, drowned each other, and flipped each other off. I finally had friends. Well, before all of this, I met Aadil and Mitreyi. They seemed unnaturally friendly, and I was pretty suspicious of people who were too friendly. I felt like they had an ulterior motive, but they turned out to be just good people. Then, I realized I needed to give things time, and at a certain point, people will reveal themselves.

"Rishika is one of those people who felt at home, even when she was miles away. I could talk to her about almost anything under the sun, and she would happily listen. I knew I would eventually develop feelings for her, but I didn't do anything to stop it from happening. As time passed, I discovered an ode within her, and she found one in me. Maybe that's why I was in Kerala; perhaps along the way, life keeps giving you people who feel at home. She had this charisma, a commanding presence in all of her conversations, and a little bindi that added immensely to her beauty. I couldn't help but feel strongly attracted to her. We exchanged glances now and then, and I knew I was slowly falling in love once again. This time, I watched as I fell, and I loved every moment of it."

I Grieve

When the earth around me shivers and swallows,

Would you be there to hold my hand?
As everything around, us crumbles and rots.
Your love is all I demand.
For when I bury myself in misery

Would you be there to walk me through?
As I look up to the sky and grieve
Would you be there, awaiting the midnight blue?
Oh, how we've grown from who we were.
From strolling down an empty hallway to living in an oblivion of lies
We're citizens of death, awaiting our final goodbyes.

I wish I'd paint the sky before I perish.
With colors of grief, love, death, life, and sorrow
With rain and thunder, beauty and wonder
But what if I fail?
What if I cease tomorrow?

Chapter - 21
Tears In Heaven

I hadn't slept all night. We were in search of tea at 3 in the morning. Noel and Achu Chettan took turns sitting next to Grandma. Tired of the eerie noises around the hospital, we decided to get some air. We rode down to the railway station, got tea, and sat on a bench for a while. It was rather comforting; we hadn't sat all night. We went back to the hospital, and all I could hear in the lobby was people mourning. I sat next to Ammama for a while, looking at her, trying not to die. I knew she wouldn't cling on for a long time, but I wasn't ready for the inevitable. I could hear her breathing rattle. It was 9 in the morning when we went out to get food. The very moment we reached the shop, the phone rang, and Ammama passed away. I couldn't cry because I knew it was about to happen, so I walked up to the room, and just a glimpse of her lifeless body broke me. I started mourning, and soon enough, I had to wait for her to be wrapped and ready to be taken home. I drove behind the ambulance that was taking Ammama home, and I could see Noel resting his head on the window and trying to get to sleep. We took her home, laid her in a cold case, and waited for relatives to show up. The case was transparent and had those battery-operated candles at each corner, as though Ammama was kept for display.

I wasn't comfortable looking at her like that—lifeless, silent, at peace. People stayed up the night chatting and laughing, remembering what Ammama was, yet something. I absolutely ridiculed how she was kept. She was an antique, something people had to take a last look at before it slithered away in the dust. I did not want Ammama to be placed in a freezer as people took turns to look at her and then went silent as the next took his turn. I could still hear her complain about how I wouldn't talk to her and how she'd recite Psalms 23–24. Those days that went by with the pomp and show that took place just to bury someone who had lived did not appeal to me. The desolation that flowed into my cognition was through multiple channels; everything seemed disturbingly gloomy. I wasn't happy with what was being done to Ammama, but I just did not have the nerve to upset a sad group of people.

Raven's Warble

*The earth tore itself in two, devoured the sun, and
swallowed the blue.*

*It still rained hail; the living shrieked,
The mortals touched the sky and pierced their
way through.*

*For when I descry the path to a mortal paradise,
My heart swithers and sways to ways unknown.
I've plodded through agony, grief, sins, and bones.
The stars thawed the earth, the rocks and the stones.*

*What have we created with the lives we've led?
Love or torture solitude or chaos. peace or fraternity,
For when the mortals slither into carnage,
Will the world still be self-seeking in the face
of calamity?*

*I see hope, I see love, I see peace.
Yet I see death, I see grief, I see catastrophe,
While I sit on the edge of tomorrow, unaware of what
it'll bring,
I rest yet again to watch the raven sing.*

Grief sticks on to me in ways I haven't fathomed, maybe because I relate to it more or maybe just because nothing manages to overwhelm me anymore. All of it seems bland; it seems out of touch. The way emotions get to me is different contextually, but grief gets there faster than all of them combined. I remember the first time I heard the news of a friend passing away; it was more than what I could fathom. I was young and unaware of death, even though it was so familiar. Alex and I have been friends since we were children. I bullied him, ate with him, and cycled around the city streets with him on my pillion. The greatest thing, according to us, was that we had our birthdays together, and even though it feels trivial now, it was such a huge deal for the both of us.

I remember how his leaving, was absolutely devastating, but I couldn't process it; it was extremely ambiguous. The same feeling went through my spine when Rachel Aunty passed away. Richie was in Nuzvid completing his nursing, oblivious of the whole matter. We went to get him from the railway station. My brother Noel was on the phone with him the whole time because he was scared that he would learn the news from someone. When he got down, we tried to be as normal as possible to make him feel comfortable, or maybe to feel comfortable ourselves, because he was unaware of something that would absolutely change him knowing that he did not know gave us a kind of normality that we all dread. When we reached home, we all looked at him as his aunt walked in and hugged him told him that mummy was gone. He fell on his knees and called out for his mom.

I saw him become someone he was not, so vulnerable yet so strong. I saw Merlin, Richie's little sister in denial while everyone insisted she be accepting of Rachel Aunty's passing; she was rather reluctant to accept that idea. I would never want to be a man of experience in these matters, yet I have never felt anything as real as this. Grief pulls on the strings that love could never reach, and therefore I sit there idly, waiting as grief pulls my heart apart.

Chapter – 22
Lucy

I've been lucky enough to have a pet. I was so attached to her that I felt a very strong feeling every time I would stay away from home. She was the best thing that could have happened to me. Annoyingly cuddly and high-energy, she was. We used to pretend like we did not see her, and we shouted her name, Lucy! She'd wag her tail in joy and bark, calling for our attention. It wasn't just pleasant for us to have her; she was one of the reasons we were happy.

Everyone at home had fallen in love with every little thing that she did, except for destroying new shoes. My father talked to her all the time, and she'd reply in gentle barks, even though we couldn't understand her. It felt as though she did. I was her personal masseuse; she would stay like that forever until she spotted a wasp flying. She'd absolutely lose it. Sprinting away in excitement, she'd begin her hunt. A huge smile would run across my face when I talked about her. Yet when that disease took over, it was a nightmare. Lucy wouldn't bark anymore; she wouldn't walk. She looked at us as though she knew she was about to leave, and she tried to cling to us with all the life she had left in her. We took her to the hospital every day of the week, and yet one day she woke up and barked, waking us up. My father walked her out to pee. She stood there for a while, stared at him, and passed away. It was hard to bury her; it was just too painful to see someone you've loved so dearly go away.

LUCY LOVE

I wish I could meet you one last time to tell you how much you mean to me.

To watch you writhe along the dirt, tail a fly, and stoush a tree
I remember waking up to you rasping on my door.
If only I knew you'd slither off,
I'd let you rasp a little more.

Every night, I look out the window to watch you rest beneath the dirt.
I've loved you like I've loved none other.
I've tried talking to you a million times.
Forlorn through this torment, pain I smother.

Come home, would you?
Take me along, could you?
We'll walk among the stars, and we'll run through the clouds.
We'll sail through wind; we'll water the drought.
We'll make ourselves a paradise.
We'll dance under the twilight.

Come home, would you?
Take me along, could you?

Hymn

I am a drunk man's hymn on a somber night.

Lonely and sad as he watches his life slip out his fingers.
I try and cling on to the cold and dark.
Yet when the sun shines, he grieves even more.

The love he lived for perished through malice and malady.
His soul withered away with her.
Through endless doubts, shame, terror, and isolation

He drags his teeth on the holy book and etches his tragedy
The nights are endless, distant cries from heaven.
A heaven they created in time
Their paradise rots in filth as he loathes in illusive tears;
Then came the moonlit man to fetch the forlorn fear.

*The man sings the hymn one last time to forget a
piece of him in heaven.
Gulps a mouthful of glory
Oh, he comes the wretched way!
He brings you rotten clay!
Sings the one-eyed raven.*

Chapter – 23

Internet Heroes

I believe the world has sunk so deep into malice that it creates heroes now and then who do the bare minimum of what a human being can do but are still viewed as heroes. Helping an old lady cross the road, feeding a stranger, or feeding the poor does not make you a hero; it makes you human, and we are all in need of human. Chaos and treachery are what this world reeks of, and when one finds peace, he fears it to such an extent that it all seems like an illusion.

My world is so much like everything I hate. I want to be at peace. I want to be happy. Yet every word I etch comes from pain buried so deeply into my soul that it stabs out a little piece of me when it finds love. It tends to make me fall in love with people and things, or maybe just hobbies, quite enough that I eventually abandon them just to make me feel like I've felt before; it creates an illusion of home.

One where love is an allergy, a weak feeling that overcomes logic, but I'd love to be in love. Every now and then, I would find peace, and then I would happily abandon myself in a place I've always been and still be content about the treachery. Yet I feel a strong sense of guilt—something that scratches this heart of mine, telling me I am not being me. I now believe there is no me; I'm just a figment of existence stuck in a rendezvous of time and fate, and yet when I learn all of this, I still have a question. Who am I?

Even though I think of internet kindness as a hypocritical act of goodness, in most cases, it is still kindness, but it has a forced karma which, at times, makes me happy. I was watching this man visit a boy with cerebral palsy, waving as the man walked alongside the road facing the boy's house. He walked in to say hi, and he then made quite good friends with him at the end of the video. I was in tears and mucus. The act of eavesdropping on a completely distant experience was not a problem, it seemed irrelevant to me. I am now a part of the problem I pointed out, and yet I shamefully relish the happiness this colour-glassed device gives me.

After I have decided that somehow the act of goodness, I watch on the screen is genuine, I approve of its inescapable act of loathing in kindness. I embrace myself to remind me of the human I am, the life I have, and the help I have been to people. And with that question, I stare a little while into the empty wall, thinking endlessly about the malice I carry, and after a while, all of it fades away into the very captivating call of my notification.

Illusive Limitation

I've painted pictures of failure and desperation.

While I sway on a thin possibility called life,
I try not to be a figment of my own illusion.
I fear I am one of them.
I fear I am an imitation.

Yet when I try and jot down these words,
Like I jot the grief buried inside of me,
I fear we live to suffer to grieve.
I live as though all this is a divine curse.

I've led myself through darkness and disparity.
I try and gather myself,
Yet I slither into insanity.
I do not understand who decides what's sane.
For we've all been taken hostage by vanity.

For who I am, I do not know.
For who I was, I cannot find
Yet hopeful and desperate,
I search for who I will be.

Along the paths of risk is joy and a vague line that distinguishes it from monstrosity. This beautiful world of details so fatally painful that it breathes itself down your throat, infecting you with all its sins and suffering that you were once oblivious of.

The acceptance of reality seems like a curse that runs you down and stabs you on the back of the neck, a place where you constantly fail to reach and pull the dagger out. As time passes by, the dagger becomes a part of you, and that turns into the very life blood of your reality.

I fail to accept lies that propagate reality as a sham. I once read a quote that I vaguely remember "Art and passion become a chore when you have to do it frequently." Therefore, it loses the very essence of passion and adopts monotony into itself and last burying mediocrity in its chest. Even though I realize this is the truth, I constantly try and convince myself to love it in such depths that there is no monotony and that promises art its passion.

I live to witness a day that has no friction to its time when intoxication seems unnecessary and life is the ichor to your divine world that births itself through the reality that you try to break. Until then, I will strive to witness that reverie that lives in my head I will linger in hope rejoicing as it advances towards my future.

Chapter - 24
What Is God?

I've always tried to comprehend what God would be like, but what I usually saw was different from what was described to me. I couldn't create a kind picture of him when he stood around as people massacred each other. It was then dubbed an act of evil, and I do not doubt that it was. Our world is pure evil, hiding under gestures and nuances of charity that cover the buried bodies of the starving children that we point our cameras at. I could only imagine the terror of the children, who were once so happy but are now piled over each other in fear of death. I refuse to give into a power greater than that of men that can tear each other up for authority and power. I fail to believe in a greater being because greater beings turn evil; they've murdered, raped, and massacred all through history and yet are shown to be kind.

If I could, I would most definitely opt out of heaven. It's not that I wouldn't enjoy the streets of gold; it's just that I wouldn't have any happiness left in me after I grow old. I would've heard enough stories of misery and agony that I would be void of happiness. I would testify against these horrendous works of my fellow humans. I do not care if I were to be cast away in that process; I just couldn't live in heaven. I wouldn't feel the pain or the sorrow I was destined to feel; I wouldn't hold on to ugly memories; I wouldn't have fallen in love so many times; I wouldn't be human. Heaven to me would be more than just capitalistic prosperity; heaven to me is HUMAN.

I Shall Return

If only I could claw my heart out and watch it die.

I retch in the air, smirking as I gently leave this world.
They watch me croak, screaming, exclaiming,
Alas! How in the cold he lies.
I breathe through my eyes, watching listening to their
agonizing cries.
I will then leave with the memory of disgust
and anguish.

To worlds far away, away from this sun
I will then find a home,
I will find peace.

To everything that begins with me, and in absence,
it'll cease
This is paradise.
This would be home.
But this wicked heart of mine yearns for torment.

Umber Oblivion

It longs for murder and malady
And then to this damned plain I descend.

I have returned to death again.
I have returned to feed on the slain.
Now that I lack a heart, I live in death, not in pain.
I lie under the earth,
I rejoice as it eats what's left of this bane.

THE GODS HAVE RUSTED

I sometimes wonder who am I to blame.

When this feeble reality preys on me
I might stretch out to grip nothing but dust.
To wretch out the feeble, gashing their tongue in dirt, in sin, in rust.

We won't tell no more. We won't croon no more.
For what sings have suffered, bled, and perished
In yonder skies are our hearts at
For the clouds are music, music we cherish.

When it floods with quivering agony
In the rain, we rejoice we carouse.
Till it robs us of our joy, our lives
But we will drown in exultation; what have we left to lose?

I now look for no answers at all.
I now look for illusions and dust.
While the answer was blowin' in the wind
I push a nail through my heart.
For I wanted was glory, nevertheless was destined to rust.

DYING COLOURS

I need not be mourned, as in love I die.

With tragedies, regrets, and dreams in chaos,
I lie I will be around in memories in poetries in sin.
I will be everything I am, everything I've been.

I won't grow no wings,
I wouldn't serve no god.
Preserving colours of the life that I led, I will be in the wind.
The rain and the sun
I refuse to be dead with regrets of love, hate, and tears.

For now, that you bury the pain that I bled.
As I slither off into the abyss, the sun will hide all of its glory.
Blood will take over the blues.
The stars shall rejoice.
The sky shall bleed and carouse.

I refuse to die in grief.
I refuse to die in fear.
I refuse to be chained in mortal memories.
For I was born to be eternal, I refuse to cease.

Chapter - 25
Death?

The idea of death doesn't bother me all the time now, even though I am terrified of it. I have fantasized about it a million times, not just the obliviousness of it; the very process of dying has been played in my head over a million times, and each time, I go a different way. The agony of death is inevitable for the living, and so once I get dragged off into the abyss, I fear I will find solace there, not because I've stopped loving the earth or the life here, but because I was banished from the colors that I once cherished. An evil act of nature in play. The creation of my heaven would be no less than the earth that I have lived on. I would create it with every ounce of love, lust, charity, prosperity, and agony I deem perfect.

I would look down upon my creation in vain while relishing in reminiscences. I would create a reflection of my fantasies, flawed and fractured like I am. I would stroll through these dark alleys of memories and find myself in the perfect moment to live. I would lie on my mother's lap a million times again. I would climb up my father's shoulders a million times again. I don't think I would grow tired of it, for it would be just a mimicked version of what I lived in. I would live my death a million times again just to feel what it feels like to let go of what I once was. To let go of what I was to become.

Ichor Peace

I've been pierced with doubt and fear.

Toiling over my existence, dragging the life I have left in me
I've been told to be complacent of treachery.
Marred in an oblivious gloom you've called reality
The world amuses and scoffs at agony.

Yet I've ransacked this world of mine
For I've found beauty in this pain
I found beauty in woe, loathing as I stab my brain.

Now that I've found home in madness
I will walk amongst the gods far away.

Spitting on the love they've shared
I blemish the heaven, and then in joy will I sway.

In search of peace
I will have killed the eternal.
I will have plundered the gods.

Now that I've slaughtered the infinite
Will I find peace?

Watch the dead man dance.
I walk into the kingdom of death.
I stumble upon the slayed
My limbs fall into a gullet of blades.

I whimper in remorse and hate.
My face reeks of sin, my tears have bled.
My wounds don't heal, my soul is dead.
A dystopian reality I was Satan's mane.

Yet, back on earth, I felt the same.
I still rejoice and flicker to music.
I still sing and carouse over the fire.
I'm still human with no soul.

I don't need empty riches—no glitter, no gold.
I will mimic life when I croak.
I will dance to the music of the buried

I will long for love in the dirt.
For life I've lived, yet love I learn.

Soul Stygian

What would it be like if I did not wake up tomorrow?

Lying in a box so cold, so narrow,
Sleeping my way through cries,
Through years of grief and sorrow.

I'm not in search of a god,
I don't need to be in paradise.

I'd rather be in my oblivion,
Create myself my own Stygian.

For I don't connect to this world no more
For my soul has been massacred, and my heart grew sore.

For you and I are blind to the cross we bore,
Every step we took our lives it tore.

Put me out of this misery, I plead.
Why do you scorn while I bleed?

In treachery and gore, you feed.
Why do you not see it's not the corse it's the soul
you need.

Chapter – 26
I Haven't Lived

I wish I could think normally for a moment. I have been ranting about how darkness hijacks all of the light and how it keeps growing on me, but I enjoy it. I enjoy every last nuance of it. The idea of sin, pain, and hatred gives me pleasure. It reassures me and reminds me that I am born of sin and I will die of it. I don't deny the indulgence of sin in life, nor do I pray for a righteous upbringing; I pray for gore and misery, for every memory shall be a memory to be lived again. I feel like all the things that I write point in the same direction. I've been walking in circles. These circles are decorated with colors every now and then to distract from the malice under them, but now that I know of the colors, I can see through them, and I have made myself comfortable in this malice, for it all roots in me and turns into an extension of who I am.

I don't randomly think about ravens, slaughter, or murder. I constantly slither away from these colors that I try to hold onto. But I do not regret it, and I will not allow myself to be dejected by the sin that I loathe. It is like a constant bribe I receive from the evil me; it gives me a taste of what I am missing out on. I sometimes want to be stimulated out of the reality I live in, and so I wonder if these unworldly beings are killing in hatred and love. I think all these so as to live a different reality so as to live a life I haven't lived.

The Creator's Death

I see an angel writhing in the dirt,
Biting a rope around its neck.

He denies help; he fights himself as though he's rabid.
The halo sinks, the wings start to shed,
it rots into the unholy sand.

I still offer him a prayer.
I offer him the creator's hand.

He looks at it in dismay and distress.
Like an infant snatched away from his mother's breast
Yet he sings away on a dying crest.
Let the son be worshipped.
Let the Lord be blest.

I buried him under the lonely manger.
I saw him burn the child.
He gave the world a devil.
He sold the world a lie.

Romil Udayakumar TNV

I live with him over the heaven and its golden gates.
We watch as the gods lose their creation.
We watch as their grieves prolongs.
We scoff as they bleed and die along.

Peace I've found after all,
I now return to the place I've wanted to be,
A place that mimics a cemetery, it mimics a tomb,
For now, I am dead in my mother's womb.

I Fell In Love With Sodom And Gomorrah

I would follow Idit and turn back one last time.

Yet then even if I were turned to stone,
I would be content.
For I rob a glimpse of heaven, my eyes shiver as
my legs rot.
Now that I am nothing but love, I wail and
I curse the salt.

I would try and run one last time to confront death.
Yet as I move, my legs crumble my eyes plummet down
the road.
They tumble down; one falls upon a honed gravel
The other chases to rescue one last breath.

Then was it buried under the mud of err
He bled as he tried to break free.
The wind grieved as the tides bellow
The sun shrieked and scurried as the moon murdered a
day so mellow.

I get pestled under the earth.
I salt the barren land, and yet it grows flowers.
I still live among the dead.
In the dirt, in sin, hunting for life and power

I will have left what I died for.
I will have died in glory.
I will have died in love.
But what did I die for?

Fireflies And Crows

Dangle me on the claws of a sovereign crow.

While on these empty streets of ether,
    I watch humanity shriek,
    I watch the firefly's glow.
    Let me taste freedom.
    Why don't you let me go?

I was once a boy so frivolous, unknown of life's deceit.
    I dreamt of a house on a hill far away.

Yet like the swing on a dead carousel, I sway.
    I now dream of death.
    I dream of blood.
    I dream of dismay.

Let the quietus songs be sung to the world.
    Let the strayed soul find joy.
    Let it twirl.
    Let the rain dance.

Let the wind whirl.
Let the blind find home.
Let the cold be burned.

For I dangle on the claws of a crow.
For on dreams and delusion,
I row
I see my eyes buried in woe.

Yet I find joy, I find love, I find me.
For I dangle on the claws of a crow.

Umber Oblivion

Conclusion

"Travel is only romanticized after one reaches home." I had been planning on writing this book since I was 17, and each month, I would give myself a deadline. Yet, after all of those deadlines passed, I would still be distressed about my progress. Gradually, as I reached halfway, I realized I was almost done with the tedious waiting period. However, the joy that one should have after completing it was missing. Maybe I did not believe that I could complete it, or maybe this wasn't supposed to happen.

The amount of joy that I have after completing a poem could never be compared to the amount of joy this book gave me after its completion. And with it came other insecurities. What if nobody reads it? What if I am a shit writer who has a yes crowd around him? What if I am mocked?

Ascending from a pool of stubborn angst. I have learned that the journey of writing the book was far greater than completing it. If I do not put this out there, I'd let distress win. I found home while constructing these pieces of thoughts that I have somehow managed to put together. I believe even if you do not find a home, you will find a journey.

I yearn to write a lot more. I yearn to travel through error and fear a lot more. But before I set myself on another journey, I must recognize that this has come to an end.

Goodbye. Visit Umber Oblivion soon.

Regards, Romil.

www.ingramcontent.com/pod-product-compliance
Lightning Source LLC
LaVergne TN
LVHW061548070526
838199LV00077B/6945